ARS POETICA
or The Roots of Poetic Creation?

The Chinese Written Character
as a Medium for Poetry

詩以字載字裡有詩

ARS POETICA
or The Roots of Poetic Creation?

Ernest Fenollosa

sussex
ACADEMIC
PRESS

Brighton • Portland • Toronto

2 4 6 8 10 9 7 5 3 1

First published 2011 in Great Britain in the United Kingdom by
SUSSEX ACADEMIC PRESS
PO Box 139   Eastbourne BN24 9BP

and in the United States of America by
SUSSEX ACADEMIC PRESS
920 NE 58th Ave Suite 300
Portland, Oregon 97213–3786

and in Canada by
SUSSEX ACADEMIC PRESS (CANADA)
90 Arnold Avenue, Thornhill, Ontario L4J 1B5

British Library Cataloguing in Publication Data
A CIP catalogue record for this book is available from the British Library.

Library of Congress Cataloguing-in-Publication Data
Olsen, Flemming.
Ernest Fenollosa, the Chinese written character as a medium for poetry :
   ars poetica or the roots of poetic creation? / Flemming Olsen.
p. cm.
Includes bibliographical references and index.
ISBN 978-1-84519-482-6 (pbk. : acid-free paper)
   1. Fenollosa, Ernest, 1853–1908. Chinese written character as a medium
for poetry. 2. Poetics. 3. Poetry—Criticism, Textual. I. Title.
PN1055.F43 2011
808.1—dc22

2011010546

Typeset by Sussex Academic Press, Brighton & Eastbourne.
Printed TJ International, Padstow, Cornwall.
This book is printed on acid-free paper.

CONTENTS

ARS POETICA
or The Roots of Poetic Creation?

INTRODUCTION

Ezra Pound called Ernest Fenollosa a forerunner without knowing and without being known as such. The statement is not without justification, for it is a fact that, in today's literary circles, his name is widely known, but few people would be prepared to say what he is actually known for.

He was primarily an art historian, and that may be the reason why his long essay about poetry, which is analysed in the following pages, has rarely been made the object of literary analysis, or placed in the context of its day. His editors have done little more than seeing his text through the press. Pound, who, in other contexts, praises him to the skies, limits himself to adding two or three insignificant footnotes, and John Kasper, the editor of the Fenollosa's essay (1992) has little to add to the substance of the essay. Fenollosa has also been poorly served by his critics. Very few of them have tackled the essay itself; thus van Wyck Brooks (*Fenollosa and his Circle, With Other Essays in Biography*, 1962) limits himself mostly to biographical information.

Although Fenollosa's name was a household word in circles that were concerned with interdisciplinary issues within the arts, he always appeared as just a reference, an appendix to something far more comprehensive. Not many of his admirers – and references to him are unequivocally positive – seem to have actually read his essay. This book is an attempt to deal with Fenollosa's essay as a piece of literary criticism, and to analyse the reason or reasons that may have prompted Pound to call Fenollosa a forerunner.

I

THE MAN AND HIS ESSAY

Ernest Fenollosa was born in the United States in 1853. As a student he was interested in drawing and painting, and he was particularly fascinated by Chinese and Japanese art. He spent long periods of his life in Japan, where he reached high and influential positions owing to his profound knowledge and love of Japanese art. Later in his life he converted to Buddhism.

The Japanese Noh plays with their mixture of dancing, chanting, and acting attracted him, and he saw in them a parallel to the English morality plays. He prepared translations of several of them; some of his translations were revised by Ezra Pound, who published a selection of the plays.

He devoted much of his energy to a study of the methods of art education, in Europe as well as in the USA, where he became Curator of the Oriental Collection at Boston Museum. A stay in Tokyo between 1897 and 1900 inspired him to embark on translations of Chinese and Japanese poetry. He became an immensely respected person in Japan, but died suddenly, in 1908, of angina pectoris. His wife had to finish the draft of his great work, *Epochs of Chinese and Japanese Art.*

According to Pound, Fenollosa's essay *The Chinese Written Character as a Medium for Poetry* was written some time before his death. The two men knew each other, and no doubt it was Fenollosa's example that inspired the multi-linguist Pound to try his hand at translations of Chinese poetry.

Fenollosa made a tour of Europe in 1908, and as a lover and critic of art he must have been captivated by the inter-disciplinary tendencies within the arts and the concern for the form of works of art that was prevalent in Europe around the turn of the 20th century. Fenollosa was confirmed in his own attitude to the importance of language in poetry, more particularly the significance of the poetic image, for the success of poem. The essay that forms the subject of the following pages is the outcome of his reflections.

As an orientalist, he was a welcome contributor to the current debate. He died too early to become a really promi-nent figure, but his essay proved seminal. Pound called it "a study of the fundamentals of all poetry" and paid tribute to Fenollosa for dealing with motives and principles hitherto unknown in the West. Later Pound said that Fenollosa's modes of thought "have since become fruitful in new Western painting and poetry". T.E. Hulme refers to Fenollosa with great respect, without, however, going into detail about the critic's achievements.

2

A New Departure

Positivist Science

"Nomina sunt consequentia rerum," said St. Thomas Aquinas – things come before words – and Positivist scientists heartily agreed. To them, reality was not an abstract concept, but a collection of concrete things, the sum of facts that their observations made increasingly accessible, and the objects of the surrounding world challenged their analytical bent. They were convinced that the things were there before man named them, as recounted in Genesis.

Scientists said that they 'discovered' laws. Thus, the quantitative data of physics and mathematics were pre-linguistic and trans-subjectively accessible; their truth is not contingent on the results of their measurements. The data are true *a priori*. "Reality" is a pre-scientific given. However, scientists were completely dependent on language to convey their findings. Language to them had a purely referential function, but it was left for later decades of the 20th century to study language as an object in its own right, and to speculate on the relationship between language and reality.

The working methods of Positivism – observation, inductive and deductive generalization, conclusion – had enabled scientists to erect an impressive structure of "natural laws" that permitted explanations of nature and natural phenomena that seemed incontrovertible because the "laws" could be proved to work. What Positivist scientists were concerned about was "the way things are". They were satisfied that man's sensual apparatus, power of observation and linguistic capacities were sufficient to find and formulate the truth about the universe. They cherished hopes that some day man might be in possession of *summa veritas*, at least about the physical universe.

Scientific problems were looked upon as questions requiring an answer, which the methods of science were often able to produce. The experiments and the ensuing results were presumed to have a positive value in themselves. Scientific research was teleological, and truth came to be provided with moral overtones. It became a coveted ideal: the ultimate purpose of man's thinking capacity was to achieve truth, which was seen as an accordance between man's conceptions and reality.

Add to this, a number of practical and useful inventions that were the consequence of scientific progress made Positivism popular and almost invulnerable. So, science was instrumental in bringing about a spirit of drive. Herbert Spencer's influential work, *First Principles*, which was published in 1862, is an optimistic tribute to the way the universe is organized and to the intelligence of man. And Jules Verne's technological optimism may be taken as a sign of the times.

The Insufficiency of the Scientific Paradigm

Positivist scientists overlooked the importance and influence of the views and prejudices of the individual scientist, who perhaps "proved" a hypothesis because he the scientist instinctively wanted to see it confirmed. Then, as now, some of the results achieved were perhaps self-fulfilling prophecies.

Also, scientists tended to ignore the circumstances in which their experiments were undertaken. Some 20th century scientists (e.g. Bohr) have called attention to the impact that the practical arrangement, for example the way the instruments are placed, will have on the final results of the experiment.

No less interesting for our purpose is the fact that, in order to make their observations and conclusions comprehensible to non-scientists, Positivist scientists had to resort to the use of metaphorical language.

But there is more to it than that. Intellectually, the two decades straddling the turn of the 21st century represent a calling into question of some of the important positions held by the Positivists. Thus, for all his pride in the achievements of the scientific method, Herbert Spencer's "first principles" are a series of arbitrarily chosen designations that are unproved – and improvable – postulates.

And that is the crux of the matter. For not only were the Positivists reluctant or unable to define their central concepts like reality, matter, or motion. They also trod warily when it came to attempting to explain *why* things were as they were. Auguste Comte put it bluntly: "The Positivist spirit endeavours to determine how, not why."[1]

As a matter of fact, all the Positivist philosophers were uneasy about the tenet that truth is immediately derivable from speculation on the basis of observation of "what is". How far, for example, could description be extended to validate prediction, i.e. how reliable was the inductive method? They had a feeling that there must be more to "reality" than science could provide and that there must be something above or behind what observation and the concomitant establishment of laws could teach us. They referred to it as the Absolute, the Unknowable, the

Incomprehensible, Ultimate Reality – but none of them ever uses the word God.

Hippolyte Taine, the famous critic of art and literature, treated those two disciplines as if they were scientific objects of analysis. His famous tripartite system accounting for literary creation, which first appeared in 1864, *la race, le milieu, le moment*, was actually inspired by his observations of a living oak tree.[2] However, and this is crucial, he was aware that such a biological model did not get to the core of artistic creation. So, on top of the three, he postulated the existence of a fourth characteristic, viz. *la faculté maîtresse*,[3] which is a fairly intangible concept of a psychological kind, including the artist's creative talent – very much like what the Neo-Classical critics of the 17th century, who also realized the insufficiency of *their* explanatory model, called the *je ne sais quoi* – but poles apart from the method of counting, weighing, and measuring.

Taine's theorizing is interesting and symptomatic. For what it shows is that, although good as far as it goes, the scientific approach cannot explain everything exhaustively: things of the mind were (and are) beyond its scope – a fact which was tacitly acknowledged, and not infrequently openly confessed, by a series of leading Positivist scientists.

Since reality is more than what science can explain, the implication is that there are other valid attitudes to, and representations of, *res* than that provided by science. And, it came to be understood, those alternative visions demanded novel descriptive techniques.

In the winter of 1906–7, William James gave a series of lectures at the Lowell Institute at Boston. The lectures were edited in book form under the name of *Pragmatism*, and the work was dedicated to John Stuart Mill. Over the last century and a half, says James, the progress of science has aimed at the extension of the material universe and a concomitant reduction of man's significance.[4] The result has been a universe where only empiricists feel at home. But gradually we have come to realize that our laws are only approximations and that no theory is "absolutely" a transcript of reality, but that any one of them may from some point of view be useful.[5] Everything goes to show that the world is incompletely unified teleologically, but still strives to have its unification better organized.[6] James' protest against the conception of the world as one and his statement that there are several legitimate ways of "transcribing" it contain an implicit criticism of the rigid explanations of reality provided by Positivism, and are at the same time a launching pad for philosophers and artists who held that reality might be different from, perhaps more than, what science maintained.

James pursued his relativism in another area in that he questioned the traditional conception of truth as agreement between our ideas and reality by pointing out that nobody was able to explain the exact nature of that agreement. Accordingly he propounded an unconventional definition of truth: truth is not "a stagnant property inherent in an idea; truth *happens* to an idea, it *becomes* true, and it *is made* true by events" (his italics).[7] That idea justifies poets' claim that the truth of their poems was on a par with the truth to be found in a scientific proposition. Later, one of the articles of the Imagist manifesto states that it is the obligation of poetry "to describe things as they really are", the implication being that poetry was capable of getting to the core of "reality".

It was left for some 20th century philosophers and scientists (e.g. Bachelard) to point out that the basic terms of Euclidian geometry (line, point, and mass, for example) are ultimately metaphysically, hence subjectively, determined, and that the measuring techniques of science and the use of the results of the measurements are necessarily dependent on a subjective consensus about what methods were supposed to be legitimate, and what interpretations of their results could be held to be valid.

Many contemporary scientists have abandoned the idea that it will ever be possible to attain a complete and exhaustive idea or representation of reality. They discard the notion of "scientific progress" as a successive accumulation of facts. Rather, they tend to regard objective knowledge as a permanently ongoing process, during which earlier results are corrected and modified, and incorporated into the next stage of knowledge. Such modifications and corrections will unavoidably be influenced by the scientist's subjective standards of evaluation.

By the same token, the recognition of psychology as a science is a sign that subjectivity *per se* was no longer anathema. It is a well-known fact that it was the subjective element of psychology that caused the Positivists to look upon it with a very suspicious eye.

REACTION

As has been mentioned, even the Positivist scientists were aware of the limited applicability of their method. Where matters of the mind were concerned – art and religion, for example – their argumentation becomes hesitant, or they simply evade the issue. Add to this a weakness in the definition of some of the key terms on which they based their scientific findings. Thus William James asks what terms like 'verification' and 'validation' actually mean,[8] and to Herbert Spencer, 'motion' was simply a label for an unexplained aspect of the way the whole system works.[9] Philosophers and artists gradually came to channel Positivist dynamism and analytical acumen into ways of thinking that challenged the hegemony of natural science.

The first decade of the 20th century witnesses a revolution in scientific as well as non-scientific areas: Einstein's theory of relativity questioned the absolute validity of Newtonian physics, which had been the bedrock on which Positivist science rested. As early as in 1890, William James declared, in *Principles of Psychology*, that introspection is the working method of scientific psychology. The Positivists disdained the idea because they considered introspection highly suspicious, even dangerous. However, Freud took up the idea, and in his *Die Traumdeutung* (1900), *Zur Psychopathologie des Alltagslebens* (1901), *Der Witz und seine Beziehung zum Unbewussten* (1905), and *Drei Abhandlungen zur Sexualtheorie* (1905), he attempted to found a science of the mind. Lenin put forward his theories of a Marxist-based society (*What Should Be Done*, 1902), and, with his picture *Les Demoiselles d'Avignon* from 1907, Picasso heralded the advent of Cubism. Debussy transformed Mallarmé's words and Maeterlick's drama *Pelléas et Mélisande* into music that had an allusive vagueness and used harmonies that were mellifluous in a different way from Tchaikovsky's. Debussy used tone in music in the same way as the Impressionist painters had used light: light is the main character of a picture, said Monet, one of several signs that the formal aspect was gaining precedence over content.

Gaudier-Brzeska and Epstein changed the direction of sculpture with the use of new forms. Their non-figurative works represented a violent break-away from the school of Rodin. T.E. Hulme tried his hand at some short Imagist descriptive sketches based on the surprise effect of unconventional images, and Pound published two volumes of verse, *Personae* and *Exultations*, whose metrical boldness attracted attention.

In his speculations about what keeps the universe going, Henri Bergson postulated, in *L'évolution créatrice* from 1907, the existence of an omnipresent creative energy that he called *l'élan vital*.[10] The ontological status of the *élan* is dubious, but individual human beings are held to be land-marks in that forward movement, which is greater than the individuals themselves. The hypothesis is an echo of Laforgue's suggestion that the universe is governed by a kind of Schopenhauerian will or unconscious force. So, Fenellosa's admiration of the transitive verb because of the dynamism it conferred on the sentence was not without philosophical backing.

The Arts

Form

Just as the emphasis within science was on the visible mani-festations of the surrounding world, focus within the arts came to be on the use made of the materials, and the form of the finished work. Consequently the artists were very concerned with the tools of their craft, and they exploited hitherto unknown techniques to put their message across. Efforts were made to describe reality in non-scientific terms, and philosophers and artists suggested alternative versions of "the way things are".

Locke's statement to the effect that *nihil in intellectu quod non prius in sensu* was frequently invoked, and the consequent emphasis on the role and function of the eye led artists to imitate the procedure of their contemporaries within science, and to analyse the surrounding world. However, their descriptions were idiosyncratic visions of "reality". "Voir, sentir, exprimer, tout l'art est là", said Gourmont.[11]

The pictorial arts abandoned photographic likeness as their standard and ideal, and many poets and critics claimed that genuine truth could only be conveyed metaphorically; a group of people having the same frames of reference did not find it difficult to agree on what was a 'striking' – and unconventional – image.

The Sisterhood of the Arts

With his theory of *correspondances*, Baudelaire had, in the middle of the 19th century, revived the centuries old idea of the sisterhood of the arts. Later in the century, the Symbolists embraced the Horatian doctrine of *ut pictura poesis* and demonstrated the sisterhood of poetry and painting. Friendships developed between the practitioners of different arts, and the terminology of one medium was used to characterize the products of another.

Since his youth, the French poet Laforgue, writing in the 1880s, had been interested in the art of painting, and in moments when the poetic inspiration failed him, he considered becoming an art critic.[12] He was convinced that a "transcendent force" pervaded all artists – composers, painters, poets, and sculptors. That force was the incentive behind their *fureur génésique*. Characteristically, Laforgue found the same motive in scientists.[13] It is not difficult to see a parallel between the methods and purpose of the Impressionist painters and Laforgue's "free composition" technique. By the same token, Verlaine called for "de la musique avant toute chose" in poetry.

The sisterhood idea was influential well into the first decade of the 20th century: Hulme took a great interest in architecture, which he called the greatest of all arts, and Fenollosa, who was basically an art critic, wrote a well-informed essay on the technique of Chinese poetry.

French Influence on Poetry

In the two decades surrounding the year 1900, some English poets and critics who in modern terminology would be called progressive, and who came to exert considerable influence on the literary climate of the day, turned to France for inspiration. The reflections and achievements of French theorists and practitioners in the areas of the genesis, content, and, especially, form, of poetry far surpassed those of their English contemporaries, who had little to offer in that respect.

French poetry and literary criticism were eagerly discussed in England in those years. Rimbaud became known to an English public in 1886, and the Symbolist poets were read either in French or in translations thanks not least to the indefatigable efforts of F.S. Flint. Pater and Swinburne were instrumental in propagating the theory of art for art's sake, which had provoked a violent debate in France. Pound wrote several of his early poems in French.

"*Je songe à une poésie qui serait de la psychologie dans une forme de rêve, avec des fleurs, du vent, des senteurs. D'inextricables symphonies avec une phrase (un sujet) mélodique, dont le dessin reparaît de temps en temps.*" That anti-scientific, Symbolist statement was put forward by Jules Laforgue in 1882.[14] The English poets and critics referred to in these pages shared the Symbolists' preoccupation with imagery, but they objected to the vagueness of the Symbolist images.

It is remarkable that the French writer who served as the principal source of inspiration was neither Rimbaud nor Mallarmé, but Jules Laforgue, who died in 1887, aged 27. Eliot acknowledged his indebtedness to Laforgue, whom he called the word-maker with reference to the latter's lexico-graphical inventiveness; Eliot said that his poems from 1908–9 were directly inspired by Laforgue and the Elizabethan dramatists. The reason for his popularity was that Laforgue was a critic of poetry just as much as a poet, and in both fields his output was characterized by bold experimentation.

In his *Mélanges posthumes* (probably written in 1883), Laforgue paid tribute to the artist's sensitive eye[15] and stressed the value of the immediacy of impressions. His wish was to obtain "l'inépuisable imprévu des images tou-jours adéquates";[16] he was embraced whole-heartedly by the Imagist poets, and Fenollosa's essay is a description of the creation of "adequate" pictures. An example of such a picture might be Laforgue's reference to "un très-au vent - d'octobre paysage"[17] or "the street falls asleep like an endless complaint".[18] He rejected absolute Beauty and absolute Taste, and he was critical of mimetic art because it is never able to catch "la réalité fugitive", and he denied the possibility of describing "la vie incessamment ondulatoire".[19] The important thing is to be new, he said, and Rimbaud's poetry and his own careful and sensitive translation of Whitman's *Leaves of Grass*, convinced him that poetic effects could be achieved with a good many different verse forms.

He was on friendly terms with Gustave Kahn, who later wrote a seminal book on free verse.[20] His poetry is characterized by a considerable amount of formal experimentation: couplets and quatrains rub shoulders with short, disjointed lines; the stanzaic form is challenged, rhymes are often dispensed with or placed in peculiar positions, and the rhythm is made irregular by the varied number of syllables. However, the technical transgressions and the thematic unconventionality (as seen in for example *Des Fleurs de bonne volonté*) serve a purpose, viz. to render "*l'invraisemblable*", which, as he saw it, was no less true than an "ordinary" observation, but which a Positivist scientist would have looked askance at.

Finding the adequate image requires an effort: "une poésie n'est pas un sentiment que l'on communique tel que conçu avant la plume".[21] Writing poetry is a creative process requiring a conscious effort. Poets on the other side of the Channel nodded approval, witness the many revisions and additions made by the Imagists in an effort to find "*le mot juste*".

Théodule Ribot was Professor of Comparative Psychology, and in 1900 he published a book that became a valuable contribution to the current debate on the significance of the image in poetry. *Essai sur l'imagination créatrice* postulated that the creative imagination works in terms of analogies. The image that is the result of the creative process has the same value as an actually existing connection between the two items that are juxtaposed. Thus the picture acquires truth status, and the reader's world view is changed, be it ever so slightly. Ribot operates with a concept he calls *spontanéité*, which causes images to assemble in ever new combinations. Although his theories were but hypotheses and the key concept, *spontanéité*, was left undefined. Ribot's book was welcomed with a considerable amount of enthusiasm by his English contemporaries.

Rémy de Gourmont's collection of articles from 1902, *Le Problème du style*, originated as a piece of polemical writing. The purpose was to remonstrate with a certain "Monsieur Albalat", who had maintained that there exist such things as absolute Taste and absolute Beauty ("Les beautés littéraires sont fixes") and had stressed the importance of imitation of the great Classics.

In his attack on this top-to-bottom attitude, Gourmont established a new poetics. In an article about the new art, he shows that he is aware of the transformation that is under way; in a characteristic formulation, he talks about "the dawn of a new energy."

Gourmont was something of a polymath. His familiarity with science made it natural for him to analyse the objects before his eyes, but he criticized the language of science for squeezing nature into a technical mould that does not do justice to *natura naturata*. What can be seen and felt, he said, can without any difficulty be formulated in lucid sentences constructed by means of words in common usage.[22] In his preoccupation with what is concrete, i.e. the phenomena of the surrounding world, he played the same tune as the Positivists, but he deviated from them in the way he thought those phenomena should be described.

La Culture des idées from 1901 contains an essay called *Dissociation des idées*, in which he "asserts the need to get away from the unquestioning acceptance of ideas and associations of ideas which have become commonplaces, and for thought to proceed by imagery rather than by ideas".[23]

Everything that is in the mind has passed through the doors of the senses, says Gourmont in *Dissociation* – an obvious Lockean echo. An idea is nothing but a sensual impression that has lost its freshness. At the basis of every mental representation there is something seen, heard, or felt. Accordingly, that is all that a poet can talk about. Consequently what we call reality is transformed (Gourmont uses the term *déformé*) by the individual poet.

Our language is full of clichés that were originally bold metaphors, viz. the happy finds of the language user's metaphorical power, says Gourmont in a formulation that anticipates Fenollosa's opinion. If we are to use style, a word must represent something, which, to Gourmont, means that it is the product of a visual imagination.[24] Visual imagination works in terms of images and comparisons, and its activity provides the poet with what Gourmont calls visual memory. Style is visual memory plus metaphorical talent combined with emotive memory and obscure contributions from other senses than the eye.[25]

Gourmont, who was a good friend of Gustave Kahn's, was very interested in the form of poetry, not only rhythm and metre, but also the choice of words and the pictures used by poets. In *Chemin de velours* from 1902 he said that "at present poetical technique has become just as individualized as poetry itself". Poets like to exploit flexible metres, and he confessed to a weakness for "*le vers incertain, aux rimes incertaines*".[26]

As Gourmont sees it, the basic form of the visual imagination is the comparison; the latter precedes the metaphor, which is a comparison with one of the terms missing, or the two terms having coalesced into one. That metaphor is a later development is proved by the fact that Homer does not have any.[27]

The fact that the theories of men who were not primarily men of letters seemed to confirm what numerous poets and critics sensed and stated about the significance of the image in poetry, of course gave a tremendous boost to the poets' suggestions. Ribot and Bergson were psychologists, and Gourmont, who had some familiarity with scientific thinking, said that all great scientists have a visual imagination. No matter if they describe what can be seen, or what will be seen, they have to resort to metaphoric formulation, which prompts the creation of pictures in the minds of their readers.

Since most of the influential writers of the period being discussed in these pages were also critics (Aldington, Wyndham Lewis, Amy Lowell, Hulme, Pound and Eliot), it was natural for them to apply the often provocative French theories and hypotheses to their own situation and to test the sustainability of those ideas in their own poems. Thus Hulme's modest poetic output is a number of exercises within Imagist theory, which was very much under the influence of French thinking.

In some important respects, Ezra Pound, whom Eliot called learned but opinionated and unable to pursue sustained argumentation,[28] epitomizes the convictions that have been detailed in the previous pages. He was internationally orientated in the extreme: he was familiar with German poetry and Chinese *vers libre*, but his interests were mainly directed towards France. He translated Provençal poetry, he was fascinated by Gautier's *Emaux et Camées*, in which the pictorial element is dominant – he calls the image "the primary pigment of poetry" – and he comments with considerable insight and respect on Flaubert and Gourmont. To Pound, there is no such thing as "English poetry"; he goes so far as to say that English poets have only become poets after they studied French poetry. Some of his youthful poetry was written in French.

Fenollosa's ideas, which Pound called ideogrammic or ideographic criticism, exerted a profound influence on him. *The Chinese Written Character as a Medium for Poetry* was "a verbal medium consisting largely of semi-pictorial appeals to the eye".[29] In Fenollosa he saw a man who dealt with poetry at grassroots level, and the concept of dynamism as it was expressed in the Chinese sentence determined by the active verb appealed to Pound as it did to his contemporaries. Characteristically, Pound's translation of Propertius' elegies is far more pointed and energetic than the melancholy original.

Pound hated superfluous adjectives, e.g. *epitheta ornantia*, which serve no other purpose than decoration. He found some support in the process of abstraction that Fenollosa used in order to arrive at, for example, the colour adjective red. Fenollosa's straightforward sentence structure with the use of simple words found an interested follower in Pound, who claimed that only "language spoken" would be able to express genuine feeling – a kind of Wordsworthian reminiscence. To Pound, as to Fenollosa, poetry was above all concrete.

Inspired also by Flaubert, Pound frequently talked about *le mot juste*: there is only one single word that can adequately and perfectly express a feeling or a thought, and it is incumbent on the poet to search the reservoir of his vocabulary to find exactly that word. The idea heralds Eliot's theory of the 'objective correlative'. It was a prevalent assumption that a poet was a man possessed of a vast pool of words just waiting to be tapped – another proof of the current interest in the linguistic garb of the vision and the thought.

3

THE CHINESE WRITTEN CHARACTER AS A MEDIUM FOR POETRY

Fenollosa's purpose with the essay[1] was to demonstrate some characteristic features about the Chinese ideographs for the benefit of Western readers, especially poets and critics. "A sheer enthusiasm of generosity has driven me to wish to share with other Occidentals my newly discovered joy" (359). In the Western world we have believed that Japanese and Chinese poetry "are hardly more than an amusement, trivial and childish" (359). That, in Fenollosa's opinion, is an erroneous belief.

His main concern is the relation between the thing and the word. The relation between the two that exists in Western languages is not God-given. As Saussure was to put it some years after Fenollosa wrote his treatise: *"Le signe est arbitraire."* In his perception, nature, the world of things, is characterized by motion and change, language by stasis. The ideographs are "a vivid shorthand picture of the operations of nature" (362). They are based on things, but they carry a verbal idea of action. Poetry is a "time art", which means that, like thought, it is successive, but it has been frozen into the medium of language (360). Fenollosa also wants to analyse how Chinese poetry "*as form*" (his italics) can "imply the very elements that distinguish poetry from prose" (361).

In Chinese poetry, things work out their own fate. The etymology of a Chinese word is constantly visible – "the lines of metaphoric advance are still shown" (379). The linguistic equivalent for this development is metaphor, whose etymological meaning, "over-carrying", also signifies movement. The process of growth is visible in Chinese words (379). A painting and a photo, on the other hand, become untrue because they drop "the element of natural succession" (363), whereas most of the ideographs "carry in them a verbal idea of action" (364).

Fenollosa feels confident that all Chinese signs are ultimately rooted in something concrete – otherwise the law of evolution would be contradicted (385). Still, he admits that some of them seem to contain only a phonetic value (ibid.). He postulates a necessary and inevitable ascending movement from original picture characters to abstract thought (386), and he sees the pictorial language as "the ideal language of the world" (386). He has no doubt that "original picture characters have constructed abstract thought" (386).

Things are the basis of the pyramid, but "stunned, as it were" (381). Things move up and down the pyramid (ibid.), but things in themselves are not interesting. Fenollosa blames medieval logic for compartmentalizing things into classifications (382). Evolution presupposes the destruction of the inveterate logic of classification (ibid.); classification cannot "deal with any kind of interaction, or with any multiplicity of function" (ibid.). Medieval logic is also responsible for drawing concepts out of things "by a sifting process", but how, Fenollosa asks, did qualities get into things? (368)

Human thought is not "a brickyard" of isolated items; a true noun, an isolated thing, does not exist in nature. Things are "the terminal points of action" (364), but the starting-

points and ending-points are less significant than "the transference of power" that takes place between them (367). The
movement is from the observing and thinking subject (the
"agent") to the act and hence to the object: herein "all truth"
is contained. What we watch in nature is motion and change,
never inactivity. Things move, and since thought, via an
ascending process of abstraction, reaches concepts drawn
out of things, it moves accordingly (366). Fenollosa postulates a universal form of action in nature; the operations of
nature are successive: man sees horse – we first see a human
being, then that his eye is directed towards a horse, which is
the last thing we discover (362).

To render this "natural order", as Fenollosa calls it (367),
man has created sentences, but Fenollosa is at pains to
emphasize that a sentence is not "an attribute of nature, but
an accident of man as a conversational animal" (365–66).
Hence not all sentences qualify for admission, for nature
knows no grammar (370), and "all nations have written their
strongest and most vivid literature before they invented a
grammar" (371). Some sentences give a false feeling of
completeness; the reason why such a feeling is misleading is
that there *is* no such thing as completeness: everything in
nature is interrelated (365).

The only type of sentence that Fenollosa acknowledges as
the precise answer to the situation in nature is one
containing a transitive verb. The structure of the transitive
sentence "exactly corresponds to this universal form of
action in nature" (367), for "the natural order" is the order
of cause and effect (368). The verb is the primary fact of
nature (373). As Fenollosa sees it, the transitive verb takes
pride of place among word classes because it gives us "the
most individual characterizations of force" (384).
Intransitive verbs, passive forms and negations are relegated
to an inferior position because, as Fenollosa attempts to
prove, ultimately they are all derived from the transitive verb

(369). Thus the intransitive verb is one that has simply dropped its object: he runs (sc. a race).

Fenollosa launches into the history of languages. He treads warily, but still claims that nearly all Sanskrit roots express "characteristic actions of visible nature" (373). Nouns and adjectives are derivatives of transitive verbs: thus, in Chinese, a noun is originally "that which does something" (373), and "green" is only an indication of a certain rapidity of vibration. The same goes for negations: "not" is in Sanskrit *na*, which means "to be lost, to perish". In the passages dealing with prepositions and conjunctions, Fenollosa becomes considerably vaguer and gives no examples, but his point is that translators of Chinese poetry should avoid adjectives, nouns and intransitive forms "seeking instead strong and individual verbs" (370).

Fenollosa's theory being what is it, the copula comes to be the arch-enemy because it expresses "bare existence", i.e. "the abstractest state of all" (369). Sanskrit did not know the copula: *is* has an Aryan root *as*, which means "to breathe", and *be* is a development of *bhu*, "grow". For once, Fenollosa exemplifies his assertion: Shakespeare has hardly any copulas (384). As against the weakness of the copula, the transitive verb acknowledges nature as "a vast storehouse of forces" (ibid.).

The metaphor is an efficient means to shun the "dead white plaster" of the copula (386). It is "the substance of nature and language" (378), being originally a process inherent in the way things are, and later incarcerated in language: "our ancestors built the accumulations of metaphor into structures of language and into systems of thought" (379). To make this perpetually ongoing movement in nature intelligible, man has had to put a linguistic label on it, viz. metaphor, thus using "material images to suggest immaterial relations" (376).

One of Fenollosa's pet aversions is logic, which pretends

to chop reality up in watertight compartments. As he sees it, poetry and science are partners in dynamism: both of them work with the base of the pyramid, they demonstrate the interaction of things, and they make use of metaphors (383).

Chinese words neither distinguish between word and action, nor between nouns and verbs (373). In Chinese poetry, metaphor functions as the great revealer (378) because the graphic symbol throws a "nimbus of meaning" (380). However, in our Western civilization, only the poet knows the accumulated treasures of the word (380). All poetry works by suggestion (383), blending the overtones of words into "refined harmony" (387). Art, including poetry, does not deal with "the general and the abstract", but with "the concrete of nature", not with "rows of separate particulars" for such rows do not exist (378). However, when we use the copula, "poetry evaporates" (382).

4

A Critique
of Fenollosa's Essay

Introductory Remarks

From a formal point of view, Fenollosa's essay is an isolated piece of writing in that it contains neither notes nor a bibliography. It is a torso, ending abruptly without any conclusion in the proper sense of the word. As far as content is concerned, it is not a polemical treatise – no other theorist is mentioned, and there are no examples of good or bad Western poetry, or of attempted translations from the Chinese. There is a vague and dubious reference to Shakespeare – his dramas are asserted to show few instances of the copula.

It must be remembered that Fenollosa was primarily an art historian – an outstanding one – who wrote mostly on the pictorial arts. What we have in this essay, then, is an artist, a literary amateur in the etymological sense of the word, without any background in the technicalities of poetry, tackling the current problem of the relationship between language and reality in an untraditional and rewarding way. The essay was written shortly before Fenollosa's death in 1908, very likely under the influence of Pound, whose interests were international, and in the context of the contemporary reaction against Positivism and the concurrent preoccupation with the poetical picture. Fenollosa's reflections live up to Pound's demand "to make it new": his starting-point was his deep familiarity with the Chinese ideographs, and the essay can partly be read as advice to translators of Chinese poetry into English.

Fenollosa is in tune with some dominant tendencies of his age because he operates with a bipartite division between a beholder and that which he beholds. The approach was the one adopted by science – an analyst as the undisputed centre examining an object, which is a simple passive world governed by universal regularity – and the procedure had led to truly remarkable results. Fenollosa does not refer to a reader explicitly: the latter's existence is presupposed, but Fenollosa did not have a particular type, age, or class in mind, and the reader's reactions to poetry and individual poems are less relevant for his purpose. However, in line with Fenollosa's predilection for action, there is a pervasive undercurrent in the essay hinting that the reader's gradual understanding of a poem is *also* a type of action.

In the essay, Fenollosa deals with concepts reflecting the Zeitgeist: nature, motion, action, reality, and language. He does not define or redefine those terms, but he sheds a fresh and idiosyncratic light on some of them. Thus he treats metaphor in terms of the theory of evolution: its constituent elements are motion and progress. His text is characterized by a postulating authority; it is not an invitation to a discussion. At no point does he waver in his convictions, hence argumentation in the conventional sense of the word is considered superfluous.

It is a narrow text in that it eschews some issues that are usually included in poetical criticism. Fenollosa does not say anything about the content of poetry (e.g. What subjects are appropriate for poetry to deal with? Should it be didactic? Should it convey pleasure to the reader?). Implicitly, he looks upon poetry as an eye opener to fresh insights into reality (as did many contemporary poets), but the problem of mimesis is passed over in virtual silence. What interests Fenollosa is the creative process *per se*, the making, which is the etymological meaning of the word poetry.

One surprising thing is that the essay does not provide an explicit answer to the question Fenollosa himself brings up on one of the first pages, and which he suggests was his prime motive for writing the essay, viz. how is it possible, within the Chinese ideographic system, to distinguish between poetry and prose?

It is an idiosyncratic text, technically innocent, but enthusiastic and spontaneous, and it proved to be seminal, not least because it was the work of a man who enjoyed a considerable reputation as an art critic. Both Pound and T.E. Hulme mention Fenollosa's name with great reverence.

NATURE

To Fenollosa, nature is both a primordial, pre-scientific entity possessed of a dynamic force, and the passive items of "reality" that natural science explores and the ideographs depict.

Nature, then, is, on one hand, the *Ding an sich*, an empirical reality characterized by both permanence and order, what the Ancients referred to as *quod semper, ubique et ab omnibus* . . . However, in his perception, nature is also characterized by motion; it is a vast storehouse of forces, and all natural processes are transferences of power, which is "a universal form of action in nature". Fenollosa does not specify how those two conceptions can be reconciled.

Nature is postulated to have imposed on man a system which finds a humanly comprehensible equivalent in language, more precisely in sentences containing a transitive verb. Nature, then, is supposed to be an independent agent, but the characteristics of this prime mover are left unmentioned, as is the epistemological leap from nature to man. How does one get from "original picture characters" to man's thinking capacity? That means that the reader's role is, to all intents and purposes, left uncommented on. The sentence, which is not nature's invention, but man's, is a reflection of a "temporal order in causation". Causation is perceived in Humean terms of time: *post hoc, ergo propter hoc.* So, the world of man is determined by a type of order that inheres in nature. The strength of Chinese poetry resides in the fact that it illuminates "vivid shorthand actions and processes in nature". The true "recognition of that" in Western poetry is the transitive verb.

The second meaning of nature to Fenollosa is that slice of empirical reality which covers the out-of-doors. It is synonymous with unspoilt charm, the epitome of the immediate freshness of life. However, Fenollosa does not give any clue as to how that reality can or should be described.

"*Rerum est poeta illustrator*", said Scaliger, and, in Fenollosa's opinion, the task of poetry is to render and make transparent the fundamental natural process, viz. action. In a sense, that could be said to be an aspect of the imitation of nature, but the idea is deeper than conventional mimesis. On the basis of the form and content of the ideograph, Fenollosa concludes that there is an intimate connection between the poetical image and closeness to nature in the sense of a storehouse of forces. In that quasi-coalescence, nature should be neither corrected nor "heightened", as the Neo-Classicists were fond of doing. It was a case of individual *aemulatio naturae*, not *superatio naturae*.

Things

Fenollosa's treatment of the concept of things is ambiguous. As he sees it, isolated things do not exist in nature, a statement no scientist would subscribe to because it would undermine the very basis of his methods. Unlike the scientists, Fenollosa sees things not as discrete objects of analysis but as bundles of energy, always on the move. Things are exclusively seen in terms of their function, which is to start an action. "The way things are" is a process, and language is an inherent obstacle to the working of that process. Yet he *also* says that "science is the only way of knowing. Anything else is religion", thus seemingly side-tracking poetry. Individual things only exist as nuclei of forces – yet they are evidently the objects of science. That is one of the many instances where terminological inexactitude seems to pose no problem to Fenollosa. However, science and poetry form a kind of brotherhood because their common object is the description of the workings of nature. "Art deals with the concrete of nature", he says – a thought that might be developed into a theory of art, but Fenollosa's point lies elsewhere: He opposes science and art to logic, which is man-made, hence at one remove from reality, such as Fenollosa conceives that phenomenon.

Fenollosa's grudge against logic – he explicitly criticizes the Middle Ages for having invented it – is that it saw things as extracts of abstract qualities. To the medieval logicians, things were counters that could be moved around at pleasure. The ensuing picture of reality was unreliable because of the arbitrary chopping into chunks of the outside world. It is a well-known fact that, in his reflections on vocabulary, T.E. Hulme used the term "counter" to designate signs in mathematics and words in prose. To Fenollosa and Hulme they are dead metaphors, and they occur frequently in expositional writing. It should be added, though, that, for all his opposition to logic, Fenollosa obeys the rules of logical argumentation and presentation throughout his essay.

Fenollosa's examples – and there are not very many of them – are all very concrete and down-to-earth: the ideograph 'rice-field' and the ideograph 'struggle', when connected, signify 'male'. Admittedly, that is an image, but it is not very poetical in the conventional sense of that word. As a matter of fact, Fenollosa's few examples contribute to debilitating his theory and illustrating the narrowness of his postulates. His poetical ideal covers a very limited range of life as far as content is concerned, viz. poetry describing action. Cases where "transference of power" is less relevant or beside the point – e.g. philosophical and descriptive poetry, and poetry reflective of the poet's mind – are left out of consideration.

MOTION

Not least inspired by the theories of Darwin, dynamism came to be one of the dominant paradigms of 19th century Positivism, and remained so well into the first decades of the 20th century. Motion was an undefined but all-pervasive force that manifested itself in the world of things – e.g. Bergson's *élan*, which was held to flow through matter – as well as in the activities of the human mind. William James' stream of consciousness theory is a case in point. In politics, late 19th century imperialism is another instance of the cult of action.

Though the workings of the dynamic force were undisputed and amply illustrated, nobody bothered to ask what initiated it, or where it started or ended. To Fenollosa, as to most of his contemporaries, it is motion *per se* that is relevant. Fenollosa conceives of things in terms of starting-points and terminal points of action, not as items of reality that are static and interesting in their own right. In all aspects of experience, including cognition, he sees "a transference of power" (another undefined term), and he is sceptical of photos and paintings because they eliminate "the elements of natural succession" (p. 363), an argument reminiscent of Lessing's grudge against the art of painting. To underscore his point, he defines "natural" as "occurring everywhere in nature".

To give a linguistic impression of the perpetual motion, Western languages have to resort to syntax. Like his contemporary Saussure, whose name is not mentioned in the essay, Fenollosa thinks that the relationship between thing and word is completely arbitrary. Accordingly, language can never aspire to becoming a completely correct mirror of reality (which Fenollosa never defines). However, poetry can get as close as possible to "things as they are" by using words that preserve the intimate contact with nature. That goes some way to explaining Fenollosa's emphasis on the significance of metaphor.

What appeals to him about the Chinese ideograph is the fact that it does not use syntax but represents a succession of constituents, and also the fact that understanding is contingent on a stepwise progression, which is the reader's responsibility. He does not say it in so many words, but the implication seems to be that an addition of the components of a Chinese ideograph and the ensuing summing-up on the part of the recipient is analogous to what happens to a Western reader when he or she reads and appreciates Western poetry.

Fenollosa is captivated by the fact that the ideograph, which is seemingly one thing, is in actual fact "a shorthand piece of action". Not only does it contain an inherent dynamism, it also points beyond itself to the next link in the succession. That explains Fenollosa's bold assertion that isolated things do not exist in nature.

It is possible to read an epistemology into Fenollosa's treatment of the concept of motion. Like the Positivists, he starts with *res* – things as they appear to our senses – and, like them, he postulates an ascending movement, the culminating point of which is an abstract thought. Locke had said that *nihil in intellectu quod non prius in sensu*. For centuries, philosophers had worked on the assumption that man was the centre, i.e. he was the starting-point of the acquisition of knowledge about the world, which was "the Other". Like the Positivists, Fenollosa acquiesces. To him, it is not a matter of remaining in the world of senses; the understanding of poetry on the reader's part is the outcome of a dynamic progression from thing to thought. No critic had ever analysed the details of that transition. But motion was held to be teleological, and also the workings of the human brain were characterized by dynamism. And the appreciation of poetry becomes to a large extent an intellectual pursuit.

Interestingly, Fenollosa takes us as readers outside the realm of poetry, making tentative efforts to posit a general validity for his theory of motion. Thus he finds dynamism at the level of syntax: the transitive verb, which is, in his opinion, the basic word class from which all others are ultimately derived, is an illustration of the "transference of power", which is the bedrock of his thinking. By the same token, truth is not an abstract concept with universal validity, but another instance of the transference of power: that a statement is true does not mean that its content is in accordance with some pre-established idea. Truth is a process, for which reason it must be expressed in that succession of words in a language which we call a sentence. Thus truth becomes dependent on a linguistic formulation – it "happens", and it does not exist *in abstracto*. Without language, no truth.

Unfortunately, Fenollosa does not pursue that thought.

Surely, not any string of words that fall into the matrix of succession can claim truth value. Nor does Fenollosa tell us how he would distinguish between truth and falsehood.

Metaphor

The word metaphor occurs frequently in Fenollosa's essay and is used by him in an idiosyncratic sense, viz. as a characterization of a process inherent in the way things are. Metaphor is the linguistic manifestation of the dynamism that is the driving force behind everything. Fenollosa calls it "the substance of nature" and refers to some "original metaphors" (378), whose characteristics are not detailed, and of which no examples are given.

The etymological meaning of metaphor is, of course, 'over-carrying'. With his few examples, Fenollosa illustrates how he thinks that a metaphor works: one ideograph meaning 'rice-field' is followed by another meaning 'struggle', and the two of them, one "carried over" to the other, signify 'male'. Thus Fenollosa connects the linguistic phenomenon with a mental one, viz. the reader's progressive decoding of the ideograph – a change and a movement. The point is that the reader's decoding goes through the same stages as the poet's creation.

Fenollosa claims that metaphors "follow objective lines of relations in nature herself", and relations involve motion. His point is that such movement can be perceived by man and, more or less successfully, rendered in his language. Most theories of metaphor as a literary phenomenon agree that in a metaphor two things – usually belonging to two different "kingdoms", e.g. a physical item referring to a mental phenomenon – are maintained to be identical in a specific respect, even if, or perhaps because, we are well aware that in many others they differ.

The point is that, in a Chinese ideograph, it is difficult to see the common ground for the two components, and consequently to find tenor and vehicle, to use I.A. Richards' terminology. What we have is a pictorial representation of a series of mutually independent acts. Fenollosa's use of the term metaphor may seem to be a bit imprecise, but, like many of his contemporaries, he took the word to mean "any picture". It would probably be more correct to call the ideograph a picture of ongoing action. The individual signs are visible and are meant to characterize by addition, not to coalesce by identification. That means that Fenollosa underlines the mental process. Rice is a plant, it has got to be harvested, and thus, by extension, it also becomes work as such. In actual fact Fenollosa calls the signs 'pictures': the Chinese form is poetical because the signs are pictures and express a picture-like situation. The inference is that Fenollosa conceives of the picture as a decisive ingredient in poetry. But it also illustrates the difficulty of separating poetry and prose in the Chinese system. For if the signs are *eo ipso* metaphors, how are *poetical* metaphors shown, then? And where is the poetical element inherent in the juxtaposition of 'rice' and 'struggle'?

One difficulty about the ideographs, which Fenollosa himself acknowledges, is how to give a pictorial representation of an adjective. Here again the idea of motion proves its usefulness: in order to arrive at an adjective like 'red', the Chinese system juxtaposes a number of red items – a rose, a cherry, blood, etc – and then leaves it to the reader's mind to "move", i.e. extract the feature that is common to them. That process seems also to be a metaphor in Fenollosa's idiolect.

As will be seen, Fenollosa's treatment of metaphor is anything but lucid. He asserts that in the Chinese system it will always be possible to discern the etymology of a word (379). However, at the same time he postulates a retrograde movement on the poets' part, a "feeling back along the lines of advance" (378), if they want the pithy formulation. Above, the difficulty of distinguishing between poetry and prose was mentioned. Perhaps the 'poetical' element consists in the fact that poets, by going back, see the items in their original form, possibly inventing new and original ideographs, whereas prose has dulled the speakers' sensitivity and reduced the original picture-forming potential of the sign. That may be behind Fenollosa's statement that the decay of metaphors is visible in dictionaries.

Fenollosa does not talk about dead metaphors, and, very likely, to him as a Westerner, the ideographs had preserved more of their original impact than they would have to an everyday user of them. Another question he ignores is whether the familiar ideographs are 'frozen' in an unchanging or unchangeable form, or whether they develop, e.g. increase their pictorial impact or metaphorical depth. All we are given is a cryptic reference to "fold on fold of over-tones" (380). Motion does seem to be operative – perhaps even perceptible – in that respect. However, it would have been interesting to hear how the ideograph system tackles new and hitherto unknown objects or situations. Does it find new illustrations, or does it add additional layers, and, if so, how?

Language

Whereas our language arose "by figurative derivation from a few hundred vivid phonetic verbs", Chinese built its system by metaphorical composition, says Fenollosa. The essential difference between our alphabet and the Chinese system of writing is that ours is phonetic (but no example is given of a "vivid phonetic verb") whereas Chinese writing is ideo-graphic. The Chinese signs are a kind of pre-scientific rendering of immediate sensuous phenomena. The result is that text and word come to cohere more naturally in that the Chinese system mirrors the world – describing man's immediate reality – to an extent which phonetic writing does not. However, he admits that the Chinese system is not spacious enough to keep all "the complex ideas together" (386), but he does not pursue the idea.

It is obvious that ideographic writing in the primitive form exemplified by Fenollosa is best suited for predicative sentences. The very few examples provided in the essay are of a straightforward unsophisticated kind, such as a human being working in a field. Fenollosa says nothing about how the Chinese writing technique copes with asking, arguing, denying, etc. There is no reference to different layers of style, and "connectors" like conjunctions are passed over in silence. Prepositions are referred to only briefly and superficially.

The ideal language would be one that preserves the connection with, and understanding of, the pictorial basis. The visible picture is the ultimate ingredient of genuine poetry, and Chinese poetry vitalizes the picture. However, the crux of the matter, viz. the technique that permits the verbalization of the sign, is passed over in silence. Admittedly, Fenollosa talks about "mobility of sounds" (363), as if he realizes the necessity for the sign to be given a phonetic equivalent, but he does not bridge the gap between thing and word, the problem that interested his contemporary Saussure.

The task of poetry is not to identify (hence the copula is anathema to Fenollosa), but to "express the interaction of things" (382), i.e. to establish relations. It might be tempting to suggest that "relations" also includes the movement from picture to word, perhaps even that the poetic effect arises out of the tension that exists between the two.

The Chinese ideographs accumulate energy, says

Fenollosa, and that leads him to the conclusion that poetry does not describe or narrate, but works by actualized energy, which he identifies as suggestiveness and what he calls "overtones" (383). The emphasis, then, is on the individual word rather than on the poem as a whole. What Fenollosa has in mind seems to be the connotations and associations that are started by the concrete picture. By the same token, he calls music "the theory of harmony based on overtones" (379). These are oblique references to the reader's reaction. Perhaps, like Eliot's concept of "objective correlative" he was satisfied that each ideograph would trigger off more or less identical associations in all readers. If so, the Chinese procedure avoids the arbitrariness of the sign pointed out by Saussure. Later in the essay Fenollosa actually says that the Chinese technique is not susceptible to misunderstandings. That is a bold assertion, however: one of the few examples he gives is 'rice' + 'struggle' = 'man'; but to the uninitiated it might just as well signify 'work'.

Fenollosa harbours a deep-seated animosity against logic and classifications, and he has great reservations about grammar. The sceptical attitude is apparent throughout the essay. He praises prehistoric poets, who "sang out her (sc. nature's) processes", i.e. they worked impulsively, without the straitjacket of grammar. The vagueness of the statement makes it difficult to confirm or deny it. The same idea occurs in another passage: "All nations have written their strongest and most vivid literature before they invented grammar" (371). The inference is that the command of language and the power of communication are healthy and spontaneous talents that could manage perfectly well without the systematizations of grammar, which he calls "the passion of pedants". His dislike of sentences, which he insists are not nature's products but man-made, may be caused by the conviction that words are congealed, hence incapable of expressing change and growth. Only sentences based directly on ideographs are admissible: they become "lumi-nous light-bands" because they emit power and energy.

Fenollosa is also suspicious of the category of words. Most of them are nothing but mental counters, i.e. moveable like pieces on a chessboard, because their contact with the picto-rial basis has been severed. Some words, however, are "highly charged", and such words are recommended for use in English poetry. Again Fenollosa gives no examples, but he puts his finger on a soft spot by raising the question whether epiphanies are reserved to, and contingent on, pictorial or picture-like representation.

Fenollosa hints that grammar is a crime committed by medieval logicians against mankind: they invented the word 'classes' "to confuse the simple outlook on life". The impli-cation is that Chinese poetry, which largely ignores word classes, is genuinely in tune with nature.

What fascinated Fenollosa about the Chinese ideograph is that it does not separate things and action. Ideally, that should go for words, too: "A part of speech is only *what it does*" (his italics) (371). In Fenollosa's opinion, transference of power is what keeps the universe going; he claims to see evidence of the phenomenon everywhere, and it is illustrated by the idiosyncratic meaning he reads into the word metaphor. The tool used by language to render this trans-ference is the transitive verb, and even if Fenollosa is no lover of word classes or syntax, he asserts that linguistic formula-tion is ideally cut to that pattern: an agent (i.e. the term *from* which) transfers power by means of a verb to the goal (i.e. the term *to* which). The transitive verb acquires a causative effect. That pattern applies to poetry as well as to prose, the consequence being that much ordinary speech becomes "poetic".

Remarkably, though, Fenollosa does not say anything about how the Chinese pictograms perform that "activat-ing" process. The very few examples he gives are static (nouns or states of being), and it would have been interesting to know by what means dynamism is brought about, the more so because he repeatedly underlines the significance of the verb. Fenollosa is silent about the communicative capabilities of the Chinese writing system. Thus, it is a fair guess that the same pictogram can be used with several different meanings.

He is sceptical of the copula because it eliminates the element of action. The attitude is similar to that of Hulme and the Imagists, who avoided the copula because it implies stasis. Fenollosa cites Shakespeare – the only reference to another poet in the essay – as an example of an author who has few copulas, which is a dubious postulate.

Fenollosa considers words "bundles of energy", i.e. difficult to fit into rigid frames of meaning, for which reason he distances himself from dictionary definitions. He does not touch on the problem that arises for communication if there is not some kind of agreement as to what the words actually mean. In the essay we find sporadic admiration for the working methods of science, but Fenollosa overlooks the fact that one of the indispensable tools of science is a definition containing a copula. One of the reasons why he detests logic is that it establishes a traditional system where "there is only one real working verb, to wit, the quasi-verb 'to be'" (382).

Classifications – another helpmate of science – are against nature because they prevent two entities belonging to different categories from coming together: cherry and red wine belong to two different epistemological classes, but it ought to be possible to bring them together because they have a common feature viz. 'redness', says Fenollosa – thus unwittingly using a classification, albeit on a higher level. It is as if Fenollosa does not realize that such "bringing together" *is* possible, in fact it is the essential device of the poetical picture, of what is commonly known as a metaphor.

"Green" is only a certain rapidity of vibration, he says. That is undeniable, but to a Western reader the question naturally arises whether it is not practical to have a linguistic shortcut, viz. the adjective, at one's disposal. Fenollosa would dismiss the objection on the plea that it shows a lack of understanding of the function of the ideographic system.

Fenollosa is grateful to the theory of evolution because, by showing possibilities of transition from one category to another, it weakened the concept of classification, thus attacking logic at its most vulnerable point. The difficulty of maintaining the idea of classification was actually one of the most persistent charges brought against Darwin's hypothesis. Fenollosa thought that Western poetry ought to imitate the Chinese flexibility in which word classes are unknown, or distinctions between them tend to be blurred. That does not make Chinese poetry diffuse: "Poetry must render what is said, not what is merely meant," he says (373), a statement that is not easy to reconcile with his repeated insistence on the poetic value of overtones. Without using the term, he approves of the idea of *le mot juste*, probably because he felt that such a word will have the appropriate overtones. That is not the only passage in the essay that baffles the reader.

When Fenollosa does tackle word classes, his aim is obviously to prove, hence secure, the rootedness of language in concrete reality. The technical terms – verb, adjective, etc. – are used by him simply as practical designations. He does not look upon a word as an item belonging to a category, but as the bearer and illustrator of a generalized semantic and notional content.

At the root we find the verb, which is the wider term. Fenollosa sings the praise of "the striking secrets of verbal metaphor" (375). In accordance with his predilection for motion, he defines a noun as "that which does something". Adjectives are one step up from reality, abstractions made on the basis of a number of qualities belonging to, or extracted from, nouns and verbs, e.g. 'red' or 'human'. His point is that nouns and adjectives are ultimately derived from, and describable in terms of, verbs: a farmer is a man who farms, a lazy person is one who dislikes work and physical energy. The interesting thing is that, in the above cases and other similar ones, a modern dictionary like the ALD (*The Advanced Learner's Dictionary*) follows in the footsteps of Fenollosa, beginning with the verb. 'farm': 'use land for growing crops, keeping animals, etc.'; 'farmer': someone who owns or manages a farm'. The point is that the dictionary does not define the verb 'farm' as 'the work performed by a farmer'. By the same token, the ALD definition of 'lazy' is the one given above.

The all-inclusive idea of motion is maintained in his explanation of prepositions: he takes them only in their concrete meaning. 'From' implies 'follow'. His treatment of negatives is similarly selective: it takes an effort to annihilate, and a negative movement immediately prompts a positive one, he says.

Fenollosa acknowledges the existence of 'abstracts' – abstract nouns, adjectives, or verbs, our grammar would call them – but they never belie their concrete origin. The Chinese system makes it necessary to express abstracts by means of concretes: the juxtaposition of a shining sun and a shining moon conveys 'luminosity'. Fenollosa claims that even signs that today have a purely phonetic value once had "the concrete character" as their basis (385), and he leans on the theory of evolution to prove that "complex ideas arise only gradually" (ibid.). In the Chinese writing system, abstractions never lose contact with reality because an underlying concrete object is always perceptible. Abstractions are attained thanks to an upward epistemological movement – the same procedure, it may be added, as that used by scientists who "ascend" from concrete observation to abstract conclusion. In everyday language, much of the flavour of the "roots" of words has been lost (as we see for example in phrases like 'the police claim to have thrown light on the problem') (the example is not Fenollosa's); but it is Fenollosa's contention that the effect of poetry resides not least in the poet's having undertaken a retrograde movement, down towards the concrete source of one or more of the words (an example – again not one given by Fenollosa – might be 'love is sometimes a meagre diet'). That movement is the opposite direction of the way poetic creation is usually supposed to take place.

Concluding Remarks

Fenollosa despises classifications, but the pivot of his essay is the relation between two different categories, viz. the concrete and the abstract. Obviously much literature is based on that relation, sometimes in the form of the specific versus the general, as we see in the genre called the essay. A poet's originality, it seems, consists in the extent to which he is able to exploit the movement between the two categories.

For all his interest in movement, Fenollosa does not take linguistic development into account. Changes, i.e. transitions, happen between the individual components of the language, but the language as a whole seems to have reached, or to be in, a state of stasis. The assumption is analogous to Saussure's conception of "langue". We are not told how new words or new concepts can be admitted to the system Fenollosa establishes.

Fenollosa takes the starting-point of his theories in the world of the senses, and few people would disagree with his assertion that a poetical picture increases, sometimes achieves, its impact by revealing its concrete origin.

Fenollosa gives no examples from English literature, but what we call metaphor – as we have seen, Fenollosa uses the word in an idiosyncratic and pervasive sense – is a semantic anomaly in that it conveys an abstract meaning in terms of a concrete formulation, as when Stephen Spender says that "the furniture carries cargoes of meaning".[1]

When Fenollosa talks about ascent from concrete to abstract, we would perhaps tend to call it a juxtaposition resulting from a semantic and notional leap. However, his choice of the word 'ascent' shows that he considered the rootedness of the picture in the concrete significant because, as he saw it, it was closer to 'reality'. That, of course, enhanced the prestige of poetry and bade defiance to science, which claimed to have a monopoly of describing reality. That same defiance is the *raison d'être* of the Imagist movement. At the same time Fenollosa postulates an upward movement away from the concrete.

We may illustrate Fenollosa's point with a quotation from *Macbeth* (I, iv, 28 et seq.), where Shakespeare shows how abstract ideas like friendship, empathy and loyalty can be expressed in terms taken from the cycle of nature. King Duncan speaks first to Macbeth, then to Banquo:

> I have begun to *plant* thee, and will *labour*
> to make thee full of *growing.* Noble Banquo
> that has no less deserved, nor must be known
> no less to have done so; let me infold thee,
> and hold thee to my heart.

To which Banquo answers,

> Here if I *grow,*
> the *harvest* is your own.

Surely that is pithier than for one participant in a dialogue to say, "I've taken an interest in you, and I'll help you forward," and for the other to answer, "If I succeed, it's thanks to you".

The Chinese Written Character as a Medium for Poetry is in several respects a peculiar piece of writing. The supporting pillar of the text – and that which made it popular and influential in its day – is the author's insistence on the role of the image in poetry. He sets out with the purpose of pointing to the difference between poetry and prose. Generalizing on the basis of his familiarity with the Chinese ideographs, he sees the difference as one of degree rather than of kind. There is no hard and fast boundary between the two, and there is no such thing as a specific poetic diction, for in successful poetry word classes tend to coalesce. In several passages he calls the Chinese everyday language poetic. Therefore a modern reader may infer that the question if and how the ideographs can serve a function in prose as well as in poetry becomes largely irrelevant because it depends on how profound the understanding and interpretation of the picture is. That means that the difference comes to reside in the depth of the image rather than the content of, for example, a poem. Poetry does not become diffuse because, as Fenollosa somewhat cryptically states "the poet is free to deal with it" – the poetical effect depends on the poet's talent of "moving downwards". Fenollosa even has no doubt that the Chinese ideograph is also capable of rendering "what is unseen", which is a postulate a Western reader would have liked to see elaborated.

The reader will look in vain for reflections on form, metre, rhythm, harmony, and stanza forms. Fenollosa obviously did not intend to deal with such subjects. Nor does he say anything about mimesis in the conventional sense of the concept, or the function of poetry. The reader of poetry is a being whose existence (and cooperation) is presupposed and whose implied function is to receive pleasure when reading the poet's work. But the reader leads a pretty shadowy life in the essay.

It is not difficult to point to other weaknesses in the essay such as it is. Fenollosa's treatment of matters purely linguistic is frequently unsatisfactory and *simpliste*. As we have seen, his treatment of the concept of metaphor is idio-syncratic, and there are ambiguities in his use of the term 'predicate', which can mean both 'grammatical object' and 'what is stated about the subject of a sentence', i.e. the content of the whole sentence. By the same token, 'object' can be used to refer to any single thing under the sun as well as to the more restricted sense of a grammatical function. Fenollosa does not seem really aware of such double mean-ings, which, however, may be confusing to the reader.

His explanations of words and word classes are generally narrow and selective, hence insufficient. Thus, he does not refer to the category of determinatives at all. His examples are tailored to fit in with his theories. 'From' implies 'follow', he says – but surely also 'away'? 'A noun is that which does something', which means that Fenollosa excludes abstract nouns: what does, for example, 'complexity' *do*? Some of the verbs he uses for his exemplifications of the 'transference of power' are actually intransitive ones (e.g. 'lie', which does not seem to 'transfer' anything), and his conviction that a negative movement instantaneously prompts a positive one does not hold water. Remarkably, he seems unaware of the role played by intonation in the oral use of the Chinese ideo-graphs, and he evades the thorny question of the verbalization process of the image contained in the Chinese ideographs.

CONCLUSION

Chinese culture is not the only one to have used picture characters as a system of writing. Among others, the Egyptian type of written language, viz. the hieroglyphs (Greek for 'holy carving'), is probably the best known one. As early as approximately 2000 BC the Egyptian culture had developed an alphabet consisting of 24 signs, and during the next two millennia that number was increased considerably.

The individual hieroglyph could convey several kinds of information, serving as an ideogram (i.e. a picture sign) as well as a phonogram (i.e. a sound sign). Hieroglyphs are stylized prototypes of men and women, beasts and birds, and natural objects. The point is that, by subtle changes and additions, the system permitted the hieroglyphs to be used to denote human activities like 'see', 'do', etc. (basic verbs in almost all languages, it seems), that is, hieroglyphs could also be used with a verbal function.

We may note in passing that, in *Fors Clavigera* (published between 1871 and 1884), Ruskin extols the system of picture writing, saying that he himself learned to read and write "in the pictorial manner", by learning whole words at a time. And Freud saw an analogy between the interpretation of dreams and the decoding of Egyptian hieroglyphs.

An Expression of the Zeitgeist

Ezra Pound, whose references to *The Chinese Written Character as a Medium for Poetry* are unequivocally positive, called the essay an *ars poetica*. That is wide of the mark. A good deal of extrapolation and supplying of additional material would be required by a reader or a budding poet for it to live up to that designation. Fenollosa did not intend his work to be a manual for the writing of poetry, but that is not tantamount to saying that his text is devoid of interest.

Fenollosa's essay is an example of man's attempt to come to terms with cosmos. It is a typical specimen of the Zeitgeist of the years in which it was written, in its focus as well as in its limitations. It is in tune with the cult of movement and energy epitomized by Bergson's *élan vital*, which the first decade of the 20th century inherited from Positivism. Characteristically, William James saw the operations of the human mind as the *stream* of human consciousness.

The Chinese Written Character as a Medium for Poetry fits nicely into the current debate in that it focuses on the formal aspects of poetry, in particular the significance of the poetic image. Fenollosa offers a seemingly simple explanation: the concrete picture is the basis of the poetic image. That, he thinks, gives a clear impression of the relationship between the tools of poetry and 'reality'. His emphasis is on one aspect of the form of the art he analyses, and he presents his findings as a series of statements of the type "it is a fact that . . . ", an approach reminiscent of that of the scientists. That, by the way, was also the procedure his fellow artists followed in their manifestos. However, the account of the creative process itself is lost in some foggy hypotheses about the way primitive peoples' minds work.

The Chinese Written Character as a Medium for Poetry is unburdened by elaborate thinking, convoluted theorizing, or idiosyncratic terminology. It is not an analysis, but an enthusiastic tour de force, which describes a technical aspect of Chinese poetry. It suggests that a similar technique might be advisable within English poetry, perhaps even that the principle has universal applicability. It is a descriptive rather than an argumentative text. It stops at an arbitrary point, not because it has carried a chain of arguments to any kind of conclusion. The whole structure of the essay is loose.

Large areas of the poetic field are left uncommented on: questions of prosody are ignored, he says virtually nothing about the function of poetry, and linguistic change and development seem to be beyond his ken. On the whole, his knowledge of English poetry, as demonstrated in the essay, is insufficient. His terminology is often idiosyncratic, witness his use of the term metaphor; or ambiguous, as is seen in the two different meanings he attributes to words like 'predicate' and 'object'. Fenollosa does not seem to be really aware of such double meanings, which, however, may be confusing to the reader.

Add to this, the essay contains quite a few incongruities: he is suspicious of word classes, yet his theory is based on the energy radiated by the transitive verb. His examples are tailored to fit in with his theories. As mentioned above, he does not take abstract nouns into consideration, and some of the verbs that he uses for his exemplifications of the 'transference of power' are actually intransitive verbs (e.g. 'lie', which does not seem to 'transfer' anything).

There are several loose ends, and his perceptive thoughts occasionally remain rudimentary because he seems to get cold feet in mid-stream. He does not give a clear answer to the question he raises in the early part of the essay, viz. how does the Chinese system of pictograms make it possible to distinguish between poetry and prose.

In spite of everything, *The Chinese Written Character as a Medium for Poetry* is a valuable, sometimes ingenious, contribution to the current debate, not least because it was written by an 'outsider'. Yet a modern reader would tend to take Pound's enthusiastic tribute – "a study of the fundamentals of all aesthetics" – with a grain of salt.

A New Discourse

Poetry

What we witness in the first decades of the 20th century is a change of discourse on the part of the men of letters as well as some of the scientists. As far as literature was concerned, the theoretical interest is almost exclusively focused on poetry and its relations to "reality". Of course the agenda about "reality" was set by scientists, who were primarily concerned with what their finding revealed about the world we live in. Characteristically, Fenollosa measures the difference between prose and poetry by the standard of poetry: the criterion is the depth, which to him is synonymous with the concreteness of the image; the basic ingredient of poetry is the image, and poetry is good to the extent that its images are successful. The quality of 'success' in the use of images to convey an epiphany to the reader is generally held as an absolute criterion by poets and critics of the first decade of the 20th century. Fenollosa does not discuss prose style in the proper sense of the word, and in that respect, too, he is a child of his age. Formal experiments in prose are few and far between during that period. The numerous fiery manifestos that are published in those years obey the rules of ordinary prose. It would not be entirely misleading to say that whereas in poetry form at least equalled content in importance, if it did not exceed it, in prose content decidedly takes precedence.

In the case of poets, the change is not only in relation to Positivist scientific discourse, but also in relation to late

Romantic poetry. Two poems will illustrate the difference, Tennyson's *Song* from 1865 and T.E. Hulme's *The Man in the Crow's Nest* from about 1910.

Song
Home they brought him slain with spears
They brought him home at even-fall:
All alone she sits and hears
Echoes in his empty hall,

Sounding on the morrow.
The Sun peep'd in from open field,
The boy began to leap and prance,
Rode upon his father's lance,
Beat upon his father's shield –
'O hush, my joy, my sorrow'.

The poem is stanzaic and contains rhymes. The rhythm is regular, alternating between iambic and trochaic. The last line of each stanza contains three feet as against four in the first four lines. The subject is a sad one, bordering on the sentimental: a widowed mother and her son, who is too young to realize what has happened. The scene is located vaguely in the past (spears, lance, hall), and the choice of words, which smacks of poetic diction, accords well with the atmosphere and the postulated time (slain, even-fall, morrow). The last line of the poem is a climax, contrasting the mother's sorrow at her bereavement and her joy at watching her son's innocent play.

The Man in the Crow's Nest
(Look-out Man)
Strange to me, sounds the wind that blows
By the masthead, in the lonely night
Maybe 'tis the sea whistling – feigning joy

To hide its fright
Like a village boy
That trembling past the churchyard goes.

The poem *is* the image – an ordinary sense impression is followed by a bold image that underlines the uncanny atmosphere. No poetic diction is used, no metrical pattern is discernible and the rhymes are used arbitrarily. The rhythm and the length of the lines vary. Those are some of the characteristics of the "new" poetry. "Tennysonianisms", as Pound called them, are not replaced by a new type of poetic diction, or by the emulation and imitation of the achievements of earlier centuries. On the contrary, the poetic discourse is characterized by a keenness of observation that transcends the well-known boundaries. That does not mean that poetry becomes introspective or subjective. The Romanticists mostly wrote about themselves, and about the influence of reality on their own mood. The Imagists and their contemporaries seldom refer to subjective reactions; a first-person narrator's presence is always felt in their poems even if the narrator may not stand out clearly. However, the point is that the narrator is not there to tell a story, but to describe a scene and the way it influences him or her. With, for example, the Imagists, poetry becomes less personal in that the emphasis is on the contemplated scene or situation. It also became mimetic at one remove: its world was *un monde vu à travers un tempérament*

THE POET AND THE IMAGE

Early 20th century poets' preoccupation with the way reality could be rendered was heavily indebted to the paradigms of science, which claimed to have a quasi-monopoly on that issue. Poets and critics contested that monopoly; Fenollosa's essay pointed to the significance of the concreteness of the image, which he held was capable of combining an epiphany and a more profound understanding of the world. The Chinese system of writing is particularly appropriate to depict actions and situations, i.e. the aspect of reality that science also concentrated on. The way the Chinese ideographs go about rendering thoughts and feelings is entirely ignored by Fenollosa. On the whole, the writer's psychology is of virtually no importance to the poets and critics writing at the beginning of the 20th century – a line that was later to be taken up by, for example, Ricoeur (*La métaphore vive*). So, those writers fought Positivists on their own ground. They acknowledged the existence of reality and did not want to change the laws of nature or attack the Cartesian *cogito*. They even used the favourite tool of the scientists, viz. the eye, and their objects of analysis were to a large extent the things of the surrounding world. As in science, there was a beholder (although hidden) and something that was being beheld, and in both cases the personality of the observer tended to be obliterated and "go into" his work. In *Matière et Mémoire* (1900), Bergson introduces the concept of *image*, which, in his idiolect, is nearly synonymous with 'that which can be the object of perception' Accordingly, matter becomes the sum total of *images*.[1]

The poets' and critics' contention was that it was feasible and desirable to describe nature by a technique that was different from measuring, weighing, and counting. With his images, the poet was able to create a picture that was as truthful as that given by science – "our" reality was replaced by "my" reality. Thus the conventional hierarchy of science and art was dislodged, and the poet became what his designation means etymologically, viz. a maker – but a not a maker of a fantasy world. The good poet was also a competent craftsman, and poets' search for *le mot juste*, which is a precursor of Eliot's theory of the objective correlative, indicates that they see a convergence between the world of things and the world of words, but they ignored the fact that different stimuli can produce the same sensations and that the same stimulus can produce very different sensations. There seems to be some evidence that the route from stimulus to sensation is in part conditioned by the educational background of the receiver.

Poets and critics do not give a free rein to their emotions or take pains to explain things – they give their version of the surrounding world in the form of stated and unconventional comparisons, but they hardly ever verbalize their own attitude. They put into practice what some linguists have later called "the invited inference hypothesis"[2]: beyond the semantic value of a statement, there is a series of tacit "invitations" to the reader to do his or her part of the job. The "superstructure" in the case of this poetry is what is represented by, or lies behind, the striking image, and the implicature is the intention to win over the reader.

Fenollosa's ideas are in accordance with Gourmont's theory of *impassibilité*: the poet is the catalyst, but his personal reaction and emotions are uninteresting because they are irrelevant. His creativity was taken for granted – it was his characteristic feature and his prerogative. The poet wrote spontaneously, on the spur of the moment – attempting to render in an image what he saw in a glimpse. There is no Wordsworthian "emotion recollected in tranquillity" here. Of course the spontaneous creative process could be adjusted on the way until the right word was found (cf. the many revisions to which the Imagists subjected their poems). And a poet was a person who had a talent of finding the right word – the perceived possession of a huge vocabulary, a reservoir on which one could draw at discretion. As Cato the Elder (243–149 BC) had said: *rem tene, et verba sequentur* (get hold of the matter, and words will follow).

VERBALIZATION

The first step in a Positivist scientist's work was the gathering of material, and the means used was observation. Observation was one cornerstone of Positivist science; conclusion – be it inductive or deductive – was another. Scientists had a blind faith in the capability of the human eye to give a truthful picture of the objects of the surrounding world. What the eye saw, was reality. And language was a reliable source for rendering this reality.

As far as primary sensations were concerned, things were rather simple: a liquid in a test tube could not be argued to be a solid substance. The remarkable thing is that, even in cases where there were bound to be individual differences – in secondary sensations like colour: is the object blue, green, or turquoise?, or in the case of more elusive concepts like the idea of motion – the prevalent conviction was that it was not only desirable but also possible to arrive at a generally agreed truth and a corresponding "truthful" vocabulary.

Deviations were eagerly discussed, and were considered deplorable, but corrigible, aberrations: it was just a matter of collecting more data. Positivist scientists worked assiduously in pursuit of unanimity regarding *summa veritas* about the universe.

However, the crux of the matter, viz. the precise relationship between eye and brain, was passed over in silence. The activity of the human mind was ignored, largely because introspection was anathema to the Positivists. Locke had been one of the most prominent philosophers on English soil to stress the dependence of the mind on sense data: *nihil in intellectu quod non prius in sensu*. But he, too, had not felt the need of explicating the *rapport* between the two.

No less interesting, the process of verbalization was taken for granted. Somehow language was supposed to be able to yield an exact and communicable equivalent of what the eye had absorbed, and what the brain had concluded. Words were simply "there", immediately available to the articulate scientist, and *le mot juste* was believed to mirror reality. For all their analytical bent, the Positivists did not address the thorny question of language versus reality. The concept of truth promulgated by the Positivists was called in question by authors and philosophers writing in the years straddling the year 1900. However, none of the protesters saw the process of verbalization as an issue, and none of them offered even a sketch of an analysis of the problem.

Poets and critics writing in the first and second decades of the 20th century use the words 'comparison' and 'metaphor' indiscriminately, and they use 'metaphor' with the meaning of 'simile'. They never go into any detail about the components of a metaphor. On the whole, their terminology is arbitrary, their definitions mostly being little more than names. But the images they use live up to the Aristotelian demand: a good metaphor implies an intuitive perception of the similarity in dissimilars. Perhaps unwittingly heeding Fenollosa's advice, Imagist poets usually take a concrete item from the surrounding world as one 'leg' of the metaphor (as when Hulme says about a city sunset "A frolic of crimson/ is the spreading glory of the sky/ heaven's jocund maid/ flaunting a trailed red robe"). Things being as they were, it would have been impossible to develop a pictorial typology.

Fenollosa is interesting as a critic, not least because he attempts to break down an image in its constituent parts, i.e. a description of what is happening when a poet creates his images. The poet is implicitly characterized as a man with a considerable verbal reservoir. It is true that Fenollosa does not analyse the creative faculty as such, but his contention is that poetry is an entity that is graspable at its very roots. He takes it for granted that language builds a truthful picture of the surrounding universe in words. He works with a simple, but lucid epistemology: what is concrete lies "before" or "under" what is abstract, and he suggests an ascending movement from an elementary basic situation to more complex concatenations. His implicit postulate is that if poets use that technique, they will find a language that is able to mirror the world. His essay is in several important respects a torso, that is, borne out by the fact that he does not say anything about how the Chinese system avoids misunderstandings or ambiguities, or how it can express irony. Nor does he refer in any detail to possible negative or interrogative markers in the Chinese written characters.

LANGUAGE

The last decades of the 19th century witnessed a great leap forward for scientific theorizing and scientific discoveries. But in order to communicate those achievements, a certain use of language came to be required. The challenge that scientists and writers on scientific issues were faced with was to make "reality" more readily understandable, to make the unfamiliar familiar to the general public.

Under the influence of Ernst Mach, the Austrian polymath, a tradition developed to *describe* the functioning and results of the discoveries at least as much as to *explain* the underlying causes ("Descriptionism"). The tradition, though not the only one adopted by scientists, was strong enough to have repercussions within the humanities.

Metaphor and imagery have always been stock poetic devices, but in the two decades straddling the year 1900 we see a scientific approach encroaching on what had hitherto been the preserve of literature. Art and science went hand in hand, science using the only procedure that could make its findings accessible, viz. figurative language. Scientists thus claimed to be able to give a truthful visualization of the new world picture. Some of them were presumptuous enough to assert the monopoly of science where description of reality was concerned.

However, literature countered by saying that the "reality" described by science did not have universal and uncontested validity. Admittedly, science was capable of giving a picture, but it was only of the outward appearance – much of it actually being human constructs. What literature could give was superior because its language could provide something that was beyond the merely linguistic categories, viz. feelings and impressions – in short what scientists were unable to count, weigh, and measure. There was a human factor involved that many scientists had overlooked, but which was recognized by some of them: thus Eddington, himself an astronomer, asked whether the world of physics had ultimately been created by man's search for permanence.

There is little doubt that it was a case of cross-breeding: scientists appropriated a traditional literary device, and the example of scientists inspired authors with reinforced vigour to exploit the potentialities of imagery. They did it not just to hold their own, but also to demonstrate the resilience and superiority of their procedure.

The current concern with the image had many aspects, theoretical as well as practical. One of them was the emergence of the "school" of poetry called Imagism, which flourished in the years 1908–1917.

To Fenollosa, language is the verbalization of an image, reminiscent of Pope's statement to the effect that language is the dress of thought. It is not only that dynamism exploited the resources of language to the utmost, it is also the fact that the referential use of language recedes into the background. Fenollosa's essay is a manifestation of what might be called "verbal Darwinism": He draws a dubious parallel with what he calls "the universal form of action in nature". The "strongest" type of sentence, viz. that built on the pattern of subject, transitive verb, and object, survives. For, as he sees it, the "natural order" is cause and effect – another formulation borrowed from natural science. Translations of Chinese poetry should avoid "adjectives, nouns and intransitive forms", a statement which would seem to need some clarification. For even if Chinese is able to do without word classes, they are simply inherent in the construction of Western languages. Fenollosa's principles would allow the verbatim rendition of very few Chinese poems. It is impossible to imagine for example, a description in any Western language without the hierarchization of syntax. However, what interests Fenollosa is obviously the process rather than the goal.

As we move into the 21st century, the emphasis comes increasingly to be on language itself, language becomes an object of study, witness the works of linguists like Saussure, Russell, Austin, Peirce, and Searle. To speak in Saussurean terms, the signifier became at least as important as the signified, which to the Positivists had always taken pride of place. The status of the signified became more dubious since it was patently different for different people (an idea that was pursued by Lacan).

Structuralism epitomizes the tendency to focus on the inherent interest of language, and contemporary French thinkers have gone a step further: to Foucault, language is in the process of becoming the central empirical object, arrogating for itself the place that used to be held by man (*Les mots et les choses*). Fenollosa's article anticipates later discussions of the relationship between speech and writing: Derrida attacks what he calls the "phonocentrism" of Indo-European languages, i.e. the fact that written language is held to be a faithful phonetic rendering of human speech. And, echoing Fenollosa without mentioning his name, Derrida claims that "phonocentrism" is not found in a great many non-Indo-European languages. The unpleasant thing, as Derrida sees it, is that "phonocentrism" is linked to etnocentrism (*De la grammatologie*) However, none of those linguists and philosophers came anywhere near Fenollosa in their treatment of word classes.

Form

Since the content of poetry was given by the world picture established by science, early 20th century poets felt free to experiment with form. *Inventio* in the classical rhetorical sense of "finding a subject" did not concern them, and those of them who at all refer to Coleridge's idea of imagination show that they have not really understood what Coleridge was getting at – Hulme is a case in point. However, we see a multitude of formal experiments and more or less theoretical discussions of them. Metres, stanzas, and rhymes are freely used and eagerly commented on; *vers libre* is the subject of numerous books and articles. All that, in combination with the cult of the image, meant that the emphasis came to be on the individual word or line rather than on the poem as a whole. Few, if any, large epic or narrative poems were written in the first decade of the 20th century. The favourite genre was the short, frequently ultra-short, descriptive poem – often little more than a seemingly unfinished sketch – with an implicit didactic intent: Dear reader don't you agree that this has *also* taught you something about "reality"?

What happens is that *the word* acquires particular interest because of its image-prompting capacity. Word and image became intimately connected. Gourmont said that visual imagination is basically a comparison. This emphasis on the medium rather than on the message is evidenced in the other arts as well. Painting used new techniques that did not give first priority to conventional photographic exactitude (e.g. Picasso); music increasingly sacrificed mellifluous harmony for the benefit of the study of the potentialities and interplay of individual notes (e.g. Stravinsky); and sculpture used its materials to create non-figurative works (e.g. Epstein). Also it should be noted that, to Fenollosa and others, truth only comes into existence once a statement has been given linguistic form.

THE READER

Laforgue thought that every human being, according to his or her moment in time, racial and social environment and status of individual development, is a certain instrument on which the outside world plays in a certain manner.[3] The indebtedness to Taine's terminology is unmistakable. Searle entertains the same idea: there is more to understanding than grasping meanings "because, to put it crudely, what one understands goes beyond meaning".[4]

The American psychologist Nicholas Humphrey makes a distinction between sensation and perception that is relevant here: realization of the surrounding world is a direct result of sensation, but our experience of the sense data, our understanding of them, and our awareness of their significance for us as conscious human beings, are created by ourselves, by our perception.[5] That means that a lot comes to depend on the sensation. In the Preface of his *Premiers Poèmes*, published in 1897, Kahn urges poets to "*donner* la sensation même, la vérité plus stricte, plus lacée . . . avec la plus d'acuité possible" (his italics).[6]

To Fenollosa, the reader is supposed to supplement – and be capable of supplementing – what is "missing" in the linguistic presentation. The processing of the material furnished by the poet is the reader's responsibility. However, sometimes the demands made on the reader are somewhat idiosyncratic: the juxtaposition, in the Chinese alphabet, of "sun" and "moon" means "luminosity". A reader unfamiliar with the code and perhaps not prepared to make the jump from concrete to abstract, might take the ideographs to signify "day and night". What is there in the system to lead him on the right track?

However, some of Fenollosa's predecessors had touched on the same idea concerning the reader's duties The good reader, according to Laforgue, is possessed of a talent for a *réflexion de synthèse*", which leads him to aesthetic appreciation.[7] This points forward to the reader-response criticism advocated by Jauss and Stanley Fish.

TRUTH

The prevalent Positivist attitude was that phenomena were true to the extent that they appeared as the revelation, and expression, of an underlying ontology. Positivist science accepted as true ideas and opinions that tallied with what their favourite procedures, observation and conclusion (based on induction as well as deduction) demonstrated. Truth, then, meant *accordance* between observed facts and a pre-established metaphysical entity which was a stable and permanent Absolute whose "rightness" was never called into question.

It was a tempting conception, which carried conviction because the increasing number of "laws of nature" discovered by scientists seemed to explain, incontrovertibly, the construction and workings of the universe. Therefore it was easy to distinguish between truth and falsehood. Positivist truth acquired moral overtones because scientists propagated a teleological design behind the "laws" of the universe, and it inspired them with optimism because human thought was on a fair way to being capable of seeing "things as they are".

The idea of accordance was essential. The general truth pattern was accordance between – mostly concrete – aspects of life and an abstract absolute. What made the idea vulnerable – and what even some Positivists (e.g. Spencer) were aware of – was that nobody was able to explain the exact nature of that accordance. How do we account for the harmony between reality and our ideas?

Another difficulty was that different epistemological areas undoubtedly had their respective truths: religious truth was tantamount to accordance with the word of scripture. And the truth value of a given statement depended – unless its formulation was patently contradictory – on the degree to which it coincided with an accepted standard of veracity.

Positivist science claimed to give a true picture of reality – a concept they never attempted to define; but the history of philosophy and aesthetics shows us that, within the humanities, it has proved virtually impossible to find a generally accepted accordance between individual works of art and "true beauty" or "true taste".

Truth as a labile concept is not Fenollosa's invention. Like other Absolutes, Truth had been the object of analysis and reflection for centuries. Thus Plato had raised the question whether Wisdom is a phenomenon in its own right, separate and unchanging, or whether it should be assessed in the context of specific situations. And as we know from Bacon's essay 'jesting Pilate' asked "What is truth?" to avoid committing himself.[8] In *Pragmatism*, William James found it next to impossible to define the concept of truth, and his recognition that truth is "something that happens" is almost identical with Fenollosa's explanation. Frege held that truth can be explained or illustrated, but not defined. Fenollosa echoes Frege when he says that the decisive factor is our means of ascertaining the truth or falsehood of a given statement, but there is no objective standard that is capable, in general terms, of distinguishing between truth and falsehood.

What is implied in Fenollosa's casual remark, which is not pursued at any length in the essay, is that there exists parity of esteem for several 'truths', or, to put it differently, science did not have a monopoly of determining truth value. That was a blow to the Positivist world picture, but Fenollosa's attitude – that truth is always relative to something – is supported by later philosophers like Peirce and Dummet as well as by a host of 20th century writers (e.g. the absurd dramatists), who find truth to be anything but an unchanging Absolute, but rather a process dependent on linguistic formulation.

INTENSITY

The recipient's appreciation of the work of art was contingent on its intensity. Intensity as a positive aesthetic concept came into the debate with the advent of Romanticism and its cult of the individual's emotions. The Neo-Classicists had different priorities: what mattered to them was the imitative value of the finished product plus an indefinable quality they called *la bienséance*.

To Baudelaire, *le frisson* became vital, the thrill of the privileged moment. Later in the 19th century and in the early 20th century, the poets who were in opposition to post-Romantic long-windedness (as exemplified by Tennyson and Wagner) embraced the idea with enthusiasm. Since the *frisson* was of necessity of short duration, their poems became short and 'strong' – the poet's creative talent, and the reader's power of concentration established natural limits. It would be impossible to write and enjoy a large epic poem made up exclusively of epiphanies.

The idea of intensity dovetailed nicely with the prevalent dynamism. Vorticism, whose manifesto called BLAST (they insisted on capitals) is an exemplary instance. However, it was the creative process and the reader's experience that were to be intense, not the expression of the poet's emotions, as Eliot did not tire to emphasize. The creative process in itself acquired significance, for which reason conventional mimesis became less relevant.

The reader's experience when reading the poem and comprehending "what it is about" may become epiphany, something seen or felt in a particular refulgence, which, when working in conjunction with Laforgue's *réflexion*, gives the reader a greater understanding of the world. The reader is invited to make a mental jump in everyday conceptions and associations, and the greater the leap, the greater the effectiveness of the formulation. Such a mild shock could not fail to provide pleasure to any reader who was sensitive to the dominant intellectual currents of the decade. Characteristically, critics writing around the turn of the century never refer to the beauty of a poem – they talk about its degree of successfulness. And successfulness was not measured in terms of traditional technical perfection, but seen as a consequence of the happy choice of a striking image.

CONCLUDING REMARKS

Fenollosa was neither a linguist nor a literary critic. Rather, he was the inquisitive observer, shrewd recorder, and enthusiastic amateur. Yet it is not surprising that Fenollosa's essay should come as manna, the miraculous food sent from Heaven, to contemporary poets and critics. They were a circle of kindred spirits rather than a school, and they were inspired by the same investigative spirit as the scientists,

They were very much concerned with the role of language, but there were issues they never got to grips with, for example the verbalization process. The men of letters committed their observations to writing in the shape of articles in the rich crop of periodicals (e.g. Aldington's *The Egoist*) rather than in books. What they wrote was characterized by enthusiasm rather than by theoretical foundation. The scientists had had to acknowledge that language is vital for our access to reality, and the postulate of some influential poets and critics was that, since we have no criteria for deciding which kind of linguistic representation is "the best", their attempt to bridge the gap between reality and language was on the same level as that of the scientists. And that is the central point: what lay behind all those discussions by scientists as well as by men of letters was the centuries old question of the relationship between language and reality: is reality a pre-scientific given, or is it something we create with our linguistic system? The poets and critics distinguished themselves from the scientists by maintaining that the "how" was on a par with, indeed sometimes took precedence over, the "what". A successful image takes us as near to ultimate reality as it was possible to get, and ultimate reality can only be grasped in terms of an image. That is the reason why Fenollosa's essay, which was felt to go to the roots of poetic creation, became so highly respected.

Notes

Chapter 2

1 *Pensées et Préceptes*, p. 24.
2 *Historire de la littérature anglaise*, p. 14.
3 Op. cit., p. 19.
4 *Pragmatism*, p. 24.
5 Op. cit., p. 48.
6 Op. cit., p. 97.
7 Op. cit., p. 133.
8 Ibid.
9 *First Principles*, p. 413.
10 p. 57.
11 Burdett, *The Beardsley Period*, p. 96.
12 Holmes, *Jules Laforgue*, p. 105.
13 Op. cit., pp. 154–155.
14 Op. cit., p. 120.
15 *Textes de critique d'art*, p. 169.
16 Holmes, op. cit., p. 129.
17 *Derniers Vers*; Holmes, op. cit., p. 152.
18 *Premiers Poèmes X : La rue comme un désert* . . .
19 *Mélanges posthumes*, p. 153.
20 *Le vers libre*, Paris 1920. It is remarkable that Holmes does not mention that book.
21 *Mélanges posthumes*, pp. 129–130.
22 *Le Problème du style*, p. 113.
23 *The Oxford Companion to French Literature*, s.v. *Jules Laforgue*.
24 *Le Problème du style*, p. 73.
25 Op. cit., p. 47.

26 *Chemin de Velours*, pp. 17–18.
27 *Le Problème du style*, p. 87.
28 The edition of Pound's *Essays*, p. xii.
29 van Wyck Brooks, p. 67.

Chapter 3
Page references are to the edition of the essay printed in Pound's *Investigations* (New York, 1920).

Chapter 4
1 *The Double Shame*.

Conclusion
1 *Matière et Mémoire*, p. 7.
2 Traugott and Dasher, *Regularity in Semantic Change*.
3 *Textes de critique d'art*, p. 172.
4 *Intentionality*, p. 146.
5 *Seeing Red*.
6 Holmes, *Jules Laforgue*, p. 123.
7 *Textes de critique d'art*, p. 20.
8 *Essays*, p. 1.

BIBLIOGRAPHY

Ackroyd, Peter, *T.S. Eliot. A Life.* New York, 1941.

Alabalat, Antoine, *L'art d'écrire en vingt leçons.* Paris, 1899.

Ayer, Alfred, *Language, Truth and Logic. Oxford,* 1936.

Barthes, Roland, *Image Music Text. Fontana Press,* 1972.

Bergson, Henri, *Matière et Mémoire. Paris,* 1900.

Brooks, van Wyck, *Fenollosa and His Circle. With Other Essays in Biography.* New York, 1962.

Burdette, Osbert, *The Beardsley Period. An Essay in Perspective. London, 1925.*

Burne, Glenn, *Rémy de Gourmont: His Ideas and Influence in England and America.* Southern Illinois University Press, 1963.

Comte, Auguste. *Pensées et Préceptes.* Paris, 1924.

Dasenbrook, Reed Way, *The Literary Vorticism of Ezra Pound and Wyndham Lewis: Towards the Condition of Painting.* Johns Hopkins University Press, 1985.

Davie Donald, *Ezra Pound: Poet as Sculptor.* Oxford University Press, 1964.

Dowling, Linda, *Language and Decadence in the Victorian Fin de Siècle.* Repr. Princeton University Press, 1989.

Eliot, T.S., *'Modern Tendencies in Poetry'. Shama'a 1/1,* April 1920.

Fenollosa, Ernest, *Epochs of Chinese and Japanese Art. An Outline History of Asiatic Design.* Revised ed., vol. I, London, 1913.

Fenollosa, Ernest & Pound, Ezra, *Noh, or Accomplishment. A Study of the Classical Stage of Japan.* London, 1916.

Fenollosa, Ernest, *Investigations. Together with an Essay on the Chinese Written Character.* New York, 1920.

Fenollosa, Ernest, *The Chinese Written Character as a Medium for Poetry.* In Pound, Ezra, *Investigations.* New York, 1920.

Flaubert, Gustave, *Correspondance*, 4 vols., Paris, 1887–93.

Foucault, Michel, *Les Mots et les choses*. Paris, 1966.

Gautier, Théophile, *Histoire du Romantisme*. Paris, 1874.

Gourmont, Rémy de, *Esthétique de la langue française*. Paris, 1899.

Gourmont, Rémy de, *La culture des idées* (1900). Paris, 1964.

Gourmont, Rémy de, *Le problème du style*. Paris, 1902.

Gourmont, Rémy de, *Chemin de Velours*. Paris, 1902.

Grice, H. Paul, *'Logic and Conversation'* in Cole, Peter & Morgan, Jerry L. (eds.), *Syntax and Semantics*, Vol. 3, New York, 1975.

Hobhouse, Janet, *Everybody Who Was Anybody: A Biography of Gertrude Stein*. New York, 1975.

Holmes, Anne, *Jules Laforgue and Poetic Innovation*. Oxford, Clarendon, 1993.

Hopper, Paul J. & Traugott, Elizabeth Closs, *Grammaticalization*. Cambridge University Press, 1993.

Humphrey, Nicolas, *Seeing Red. A Study in Consciousness*. Cambridge, Mass.: The Belknap Press of Harvard University Press, 2006.

James, William, *Pragmatism*. New York, 1907.

James, William, *Pragmatism and Other Writings*. New York, Penguin Putnam 2000.

Kahn, Gustave, *Premiers Poèmes*. Paris, 1897.

Kahn, Gustave, *Le vers libre*. Paris, 1912.

Kaplan, Carola M. & Simpson, Anne B. (eds.), *Seeing Double: Revisioning Edwardian and Modern Literature*. New York, 1996.

Kasper, John (ed.), *The Chinese Written Character as a Medium for Poetry*. New York, 1992.

Kenner, Hugh, *The Pound Era*. Berkeley, University of California Press, 1974.

Kern, Stephen, *The Culture of Time and Space, 1880–1914*. Harvard University Press, 1983.

Laforgue, Jules, *Oeuvres complètes*. Paris, 1922.

Laforgue, Jules, *Mélanges posthumes* (ed. P. Bonnefis). Paris, 1979. Doltin, Presses Universitaires de Lille, 1993.

Laforgue, Jules, *Textes de critique d'art*. Réunis et présentés par Mireille Doltin, Presses Universitaires de Lille, 1993.

McDougal, Stuart, *Ezra Pound and the Troubadour Tradition*. Princeton University Press, 1972.

Materer, Timothy, *Vortex: Pound, Eliot, and Lewis.* Cornell University Press, 1979.

Mellon, James R., *Charmed Circle: Gertrude Stein and Company.* New York, 1974.

Mesthrie, Rajend, Swann, Joan, Deumert, Andrea & Leap, William L., *Introducing Sociolinguistics.* Edinburgh University Press, 2000.

Nagy, N. Christoph de, *Ezra Pound's Poetics and Literary Tradition.* Bern (Francke), 1966.

Olsen, Flemming, *Between Positivism and T.S. Eliot: Imagism and T.E. Hulme.* University Press of Southern Denmark, 2008.

Pearson, Karl, *The Grammar of Science.* London, 1892.

Pinker, Steven, *The Stuff of Thought. Language as a Window into Human Nature.* Allen Lane, 2007.

Pound, Ezra, *Lustra.* London, 1916.

Pound, Ezra, *Personae and Exultations.* London, 1913.

Pound, Ezra, *Make It New.* London, 1934.

Pound, Ezra, *Literary Essays* (ed. T.S. Eliot). London, 1960.

Ribot, Théophile, *Essai sur l'imagination créatrice.* Paris, 1900.

Richards, I.A., 'The Poetry of T.S. Eliot' (1926) in *Principles of Literary Criticism,* 2nd ed., New York, 1928.

Ricoeur, Paul, *La métaphore vive.* Paris, 1975.

Russell, Bertrand, *On Denoting.* Cambridge University Press, 1905.

Schneidan, Herbert, *Ezra Pound: The Image and the Real.* Baton Rouge, Louisiana State University Press, 1969.

Scott, Clive, *Vers libre.* Oxford University Press, 1990.

Searle, John, *Intentionality. An Essay in the Philosophy of Mind.* Cambridge University Press, 1983.

Sherry, Vincent, *The Great War and the Language of Modernism.* Oxford University Press, 2003.

Sieburth, Richard, *Investigations. Ezra Pound and Rémy de Gourmont.* Harvard University Press, 1978.

Stein, Gertrude, *Bee Vine and other Pieces (1913–27).* Yale University Press, 1953.

Stein, Gertrude, *Painted Lace and Other Pieces (1914–37).* Yale University Press, 1955.

Taine Hyppolyte, *Philosophie de l'art*. Corpus des oeuvres de philosophie de langue française. Texte revu par Stéphane Douailler. Fayard, 1985.

Taupin, René, *L'influence du symbolisme français sur la poésie américaine (de 1910 à 1920)*. Paris, 1920.

Traugott, Elizabeth Closs & Dasher, Richard, *Regularity in Semantic Change*. Cambridge University Press, 2000.

Vaihinger, Hans, *The Philosophy of 'As If': A System of Theoretical and Religious Fictions of Mankind* (trans. C.K. Ogden, 1935); repr. New York, 1966.

Wees, William, *Vorticism and the English Avant-Garde*. University of Toronto Press, 1972.

Whitworth, Michael H., *Einstein's Wake. Relativity, Metaphor, and Modernist Literature*. Oxford University Press, 2001.

Wittgenstein, Ludwig, *Tractatus logico-philosophicus*. Cambridge University Press, 1922.

Wittgenstein, Ludwig, *Philosophische Untersuchungen*. Cambridge University Press, 1953.

INDEX

abstract/abstraction, 19, 21, 23, 29,
   32, 40, 41, 42, 43, 45, 48, 56, 61,
   62
accordance, 6, 32, 61, 62
action, 20, 21, 22, 23, 24,, 26, 27, 28,
   29, 30 34, 38, 39
adjective, 19, 23, 34, 40, 41, 58
agent, 28, 38
Albalat, 16
Aldington, 18, 65
Aquinas, St. Thomas, 5
argumentation, 26, 30, 48
Aristotle, 55
ars poetica, 47
ascent, 21, 22, 32, 41, 43, 56
association, 37
Austin, 58

Bachelard, 9
Bacon, 62
Baudelaire, 13, 63
beauty, 15, 16, 62, 64
beholder, 26, 52
Bergson, 11, 18, 30, 52
bienséance, 63
BLAST, 64
Bohr, 7
Buddhism, 3

Cato the Elder, 54
cause, 22, 28, 58
change, 20, 22, 33, 37, 42, 46, 48, 50
Classics, 16
classification, 21, 37, 39, 40, 42

Coleridge, 59
communication, 37, 39
Comte, Auguste, 7
comparison, 53, 55, 60
concept, 21, 22, 26, 37, 42, 54, 55,
   62
conclusion, 5, 25, 42, 54, 61
concrete, 21, 24, 29, 30, 37, 41, 43,
   47, 49, 52, 56, 61, 62
conjunction, 23
connotation, 37
content, 25, 26, 28, 30, 32, 40, 44, 45,
   50, 59
copula, 23, 24, 25, 36, 39
counter, 29, 38
Cubism, 11

Darwin, 30, 40, 58
Debussy, 11
deduction, 5, 54, 61
Derrida, 59
Descartes, 52
description, 7, 8, 29, 30, 37, 48, 51,
   56, 59
didacticism, 26, 59
Ding an sich, 27
Dummet, 63
dynamism, 19, 24, 27, 30, 31, 32, 33,
   39, 58

Eddington, 57
effect, 22, 58
Einstein, 11
élan, 30